Pebble®

Some Kids Wear Leg Braces

Revised and Updated

by Lola M. Schaefer

Consulting Editor: Gail Saunders-Smith, PhD

Consultant: Nancy Dobson, Director
Pediatric Therapy Services, Mankato, Minnesota

Capstone press®

Mankato, Minnesota

Pebble Books are published by Capstone Press,
1710 Roe Crest Drive, North Mankato, Minnesota 56003.
www.capstonepub.com

Library of Congress Cataloging-in-Publication Data
Schaefer, Lola M., 1950–
    Some kids wear leg braces / by Lola M. Schaefer.—Rev. and updated.
    p. cm.—(Pebble books. Understanding differences)
    Includes bibliographical references and index.
    ISBN: 978-1-4296-0813-8 (hardcover)
    ISBN: 978-1-4296-1777-2 (softcover)
    1. Children with disabilities—Juvenile literature. 2. Orthopedic braces—Juvenile
literature. 3. Leg—Abnormalities—Juvenile literature. I. Title. II. Series.
HV903.S33 2008
362.4'3—dc22   2007009117

Summary: Describes some of the reasons children might wear leg braces and how
leg braces are helpful.

Note to Parents and Teachers

The Understanding Differences set supports national social
studies standards related to individual development and identity.
This book describes and illustrates the special needs of children
who wear leg braces. The photographs support early readers in
understanding the text. The repetition of words and phrases helps
early readers learn new words. This book also introduces early
readers to subject-specific vocabulary words, which are defined
in the Glossary. Early readers may need assistance to read some
words and to use the Table of Contents, Glossary, Read More,
Internet Sites, and Index sections of the book.

Printed in the United States   4643

Table of Contents

How Leg Braces Help

Some kids wear leg braces.
Leg braces support
weak or injured legs.
Leg braces help kids
stand and move.

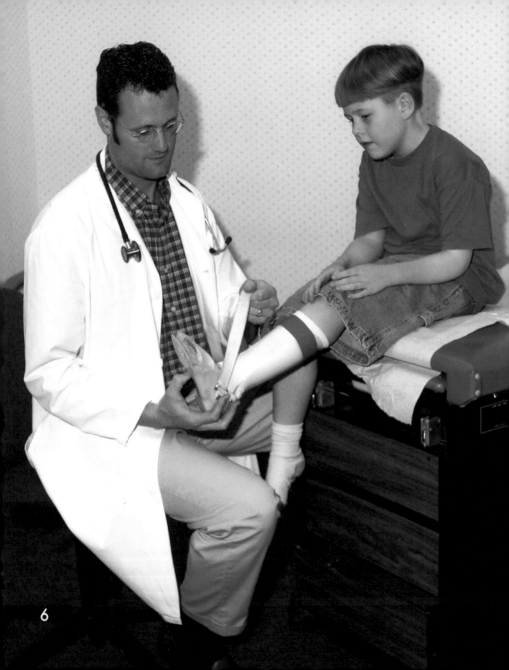

Some kids who wear
leg braces are born with
weak bones or muscles.
Other kids wear leg braces
because they got hurt.

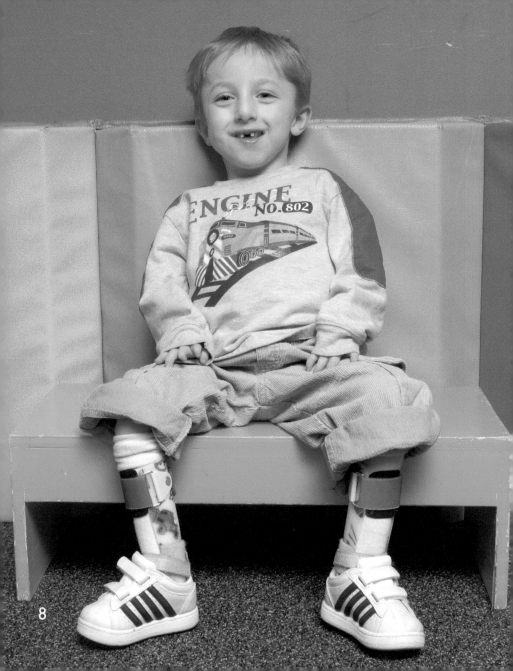

Some kids start wearing leg braces when they are very young.

Leg braces are different
colors and sizes.
Leg braces cover
the whole leg or
only part of the leg.

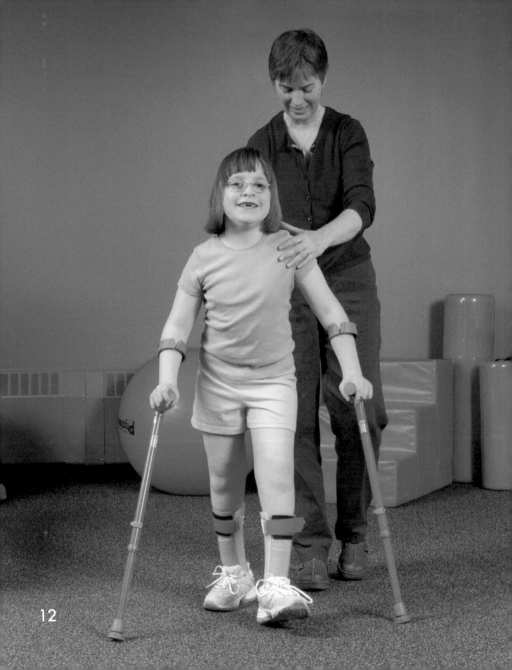

Physical therapists teach kids to use leg braces. They teach kids how to exercise and move.

Everyday Life

Some kids who wear
leg braces use walkers
or crutches.
They go for walks.

Kids who wear leg braces help at home.
They dust or do other jobs.

Kids who wear leg braces
enjoy animals.
They take care of
their pets.

Kids who wear leg braces like to have fun.
They play with their friends.

Glossary

crutch—a long wooden or metal stick with a padded top; people with leg injuries often use crutches to help them walk.

exercise—physical activity that a person does to keep fit and healthy

injured—damaged or hurt; some people wear leg braces because they were injured.

physical therapist—a person trained to give treatment to people who are hurt or have physical disabilities; massage and exercise are two kinds of treatment.

support—to help hold something in place; leg braces support weak joints and injured legs and feet.

walker—a metal frame with four legs and wheels that supports people when they walk; walkers improve balance and stability.

Read More

Dwight, Laura. *Brothers and Sisters.* New York: Star Bright Books, 2005.

Schaefer, Adam. *Tools that Help Me.* The World around Me. Vero Beach, Fla,: Rourke, 2007.

Thomas, Pat. *Don't Call Me Special: A First Look at Disability.* New York: Barron's, 2002.

Internet Sites

FactHound offers a safe, fun way to find Internet sites related to this book. All of the sites on FactHound have been researched by our staff.

Here's how:

1. Visit *www.facthound.com*

2. Choose your grade level.

3. Type in this book ID **1429608137** for age-appropriate sites. You may also browse subjects by clicking on letters, or by clicking on pictures and words.

4. Click on the **Fetch It** button.

FactHound will fetch the best sites for you!　　　23

Index

Word Count: 142

Early-Intervention Level: 13

Editorial Credits

Rebecca Glaser, revised edition editor; Mari C. Schuh, editor; Bob Lentz, revised
edition designer; Katy Kudela, photo researcher; Kelly Garvin, photo stylist

Photo Credits

Capstone Press/Karon Dubke, cover, 4, 8, 10, 12, 14, 16, 20
Gregg R. Andersen, 6
Muscular Dystrophy Association, 18

Capstone Press thanks Nancy Dobson and the staff of Pediatric Therapy Services in
Mankato, Minnesota, for their assistance with photographs for this book.